ZUFAN...
AND THE FLOWER

AUTHOR: **HAYMANOT BERHANU**

GRAPHIC DESIGN & LAYOUT: **H. W. STONE**

ILLUSTRATOR: **SOLOMON G. KITAW**

ZUFAN...
AND THE FLOWER

ISBN: 97809713758-4-4
Author's North American Edition

Written by Haymanot Berhanu
Editing and Graphic Design by H. W. Stone
©2007 all rights reserved

Illustrations by Solomon G. Kitaw
Spanish Translation by Rosana Farias
French Translation by Luc Guglielmi
Prepress by Imaging Hawaii

ትንሽ ልጅ ሳለሁ ዙፋን ብዙ ጊዜ ችግር ውስጥ ትገባ ነበር፡ ዙፋን ሁሌ በራሷ መንገድ ማድረግና ምን ያህል መግፋት እንደምትችል መፈተን ትሞክራለች።

When I was a small child my sister Zufan used to get into trouble a lot. Zufan always wanted to do things her way, and she always tried to see what she could get away with.

Quand j'étais petite fille, ma sœur Zufan avait l'habitude de s'attirer des ennuis. Zufan voulait toujours faire ce qu'elle voulait sans demander l'avis de personne. Elle essayait toujours de savoir jusqu'où elle pouvait aller sans se faire gronder

Cuando yo era pequeña, mi hermanita Zufán siempre se metía en problemas. Zufán siempre quería hacer las cosas a su manera, y siempre trataba de ver la forma de salirse con la suya.

ከእለታት አንድ ቀን ዙፋን ትንሽ ልጅ ሳለች ለእናታችን ስጦታ ለመስጠት ፈለገች። እደጃችን የተተከሉ የሚያማምሩ አበባዎች ነበሩ። አባታችን አበቦቹን እንዳትነካ ደጋግሞ አስጠንቅቋት ነበር።

One day, when Zufan was very young, she decided she wanted to give our mother a present. Outside our door was a garden where we had planted flowers, very beautiful flowers, flowers her father had warned her to leave alone, flowers he told her not even to touch.

Un jour, quand Zufan était encore très jeune, elle décida qu'elle voulait offrir un cadeau à notre mère. A l'extérieur, il y avait un jardin magnifique où était planté des fleurs, de très jolies fleurs, des fleurs dont notre père nous avait mis en garde de ne pas s'aventurer trop près et certainement de ne pas toucher.

Un día cuando Zufán era aún muy pequeña, decidió que quería darle a nuestra mamá un regalo. Afuera de la casa estaba el jardín donde habíamos plantado flores, flores muy bonitas, y su papá le había dicho que las dejara en paz, que ni siquiera las tocara.

ዙፋን ለእናታችን ስጦታ ለመስጠት ስለፈለገች ተደብቃ ወደ አበባዎቹ መደብ ሄደች። ከሁሉም ያማረችውን አበባ ቀጠፈችና እናታችንን ፍለጋ ሄደች። እናታችንና አጎታችን ዮሃንስ በረንዳ ላይ ቁጭ ብለው ይጫወቱ ነበር። ዙፋንም የቀጠፈችውን አበባ ከጀርባዋ ደብቃ ወደ በረንዳው ቀረበች "እማዬ በእጄ ምን እንደያዝኩ ታውቂያለሽ?" ስትል እናታችንን ጠየቀች።

Because she wanted to give her mother a special present Zufan sneaked out to the flower bed when no one was watching and pulled up the most beautiful flower in the flower bed, and then went looking for her mother. When she found her, Zufan hid the flower behind her back and went over to where her mother was sitting on the porch, talking with Uncle Yohannes. Zufan shyly asked her mother "Guess what I have in my hand?"

Comme elle voulait offrir à sa mère un très jolie cadeau, Zufan pénétra sans rien dire dans le jardin et en cueilli la plus jolie fleur. Elle alla ensuite chercher sa mère, cachant la fleur cueillie derrière son dos. Elle trouva sa mère parlant avec son oncle Yohannes sur les marches de l'escalier. Zufan demanda timidement à sa mère : " Devine ce que je cache derrière mon dos ? "

Como Zufán quería darle a mamá un regalo muy especial, se salió al jardín cuando nadie la estaba viendo, cortó la flor más bonita de todo el jardín y fue a buscar a mamá. Cuando la encontró, Zufán escondió la flor detrás de ella y se acercó a mamá, quien estaba sentada en el portal platicando con el Tío Yohannes. Tímidamente Zufán le dijo a mamá: ¡Adivina lo que traigo en la mano!

እናታችንም በፈገግታ “ምንድነው? ብላ ጠየቀች። ዙፋንም “አበባ ነው ለአንቺ እማዬ” ብላ እጇን ዘረጋች። እናታችንም “አይሆንም! ለምን አበባውን ቀጠፍሽ? አባትሽ ሲመጣ ጉድሽ ይፈላል!” አለቻት።

Her mother smiled and asked Zufan "What is it?" "It is a flower for you, mommy!" Zufan said as she pulled the flower from where it was hidden behind her back, giving it to her mother. Zufan's mother was very upset. "Oh no! Why did you pull up that flower?" Her mother exclaimed. "You will be in big trouble when your father sees it!"

Sa mère sourit et demanda à Zufan, " Qu'est-ce que c'est ? " " C'est une fleur pour toi, maman ! " dit Zufan en montrant la fleur qu'elle cachait derrière son dos et la donnant à sa mère. La mère de Zufan était très fâchée. " Oh non !!! Pourquoi as-tu cueilli cette fleur ? " Lui cria sa mère. " Ton père sera très fâché quand il découvrira ce que tu as fait ! "

Su mamá sonrió y le preguntó a Zufán: "¿Qué es?". "Es una flor para ti mamá," le dijo Zufán mientras le entregaba la flor a su mamá. La mamá se molestó mucho. "¡Oh, no! ¿Por qué arrancaste esa flor?" Exclamó su mamá. "¡Cuando tu papá la vea se va a molestar mucho contigo!"

ይህን ስትሰማ ዙፋን ፈራች፡ ምን ማድረግ እንዳለባት አላወቀችም ነበር። ዙፋን አባታችን እነደሚወዳት ታውቃለች ትእዛዙን እነደጣሰች ተገንዝባ በፍራቻ መንፈስ ተዋጠች።

When she heard this Zufan became afraid, and did not know what to do. Zufan knew her father loved her, but she also knew that she had disobeyed him, and pulled up the flower that he had told her not to touch.

Quand elle entendit cela, Zufan eut peur et elle ne savait que faire. Zufan savait que son père l'aimait mais elle savait également qu'elle lui avait désobéi en cueillant une des fleurs alors qu'il lui avait dit de ne jamais les toucher.

Cuando Zufán escuchó esto le dio mucho miedo y no supo qué hacer. Ella sabía que su papá la quería, pero también sabía que lo había desobedecido al arrancar una flor del jardín que no debía tocar.

ዙፋን ስለፈራችም መሮጥ ጀመረች፣ ማንም ግን ያስተዋለ ሰው አልነበረም። ትናንሽ ልጆች ሁሌም ይጫወታሉ፣ ይሮጣሉ ስለዚህ ማንም ሰው እየተጫወተች እንዳልነበር አላስተዋለም።

Because she was afraid Zufan started running, but no one paid any attention to her because small children run and play all the time, and no one realized that Zufan was not just playing.

Parce qu'elle était très effrayée, Zufan commença à courir, mais personne ne fit attention à elle parce que tous les enfants courent et jouent. Personne ne réalisa que Zufan ne jouait pas.

Como Zufán tenía miedo, comenzó a correr, pero nadie le prestó mucha atención porque los niños pequeños corren y juegan todo el tiempo, y nadie se dio cuenta de que Zufán no estaba solamente jugando.

ዙፋን የአባቷን ትዕዛዝ አለማክበሯንና ቅጣቷን ስለፈራች መሀል ሜዳ ላይ ቆማ ከሩቅ የሚታያት ከአንድ አሮጌ የቁም ሳጥን ላይ አተኮረች። “እዚህ ውስጥ ነው የምደበቀው” አለች።

Sad because she realized she had disobeyed her father, and afraid she was going to be punished, Zufan was standing in the courtyard when she saw an old, empty cupboard. Zufan looked at it, and then said to herself, "That is where I am going to hide."

Triste parce qu'elle réalisa qu'elle avait désobéi à son père, et effrayée d'être punie, Zufan restait debout dans la cour quand elle aperçu un vieux carton vide. Zufan le regarda et se dit : " C'est là-dedans que je vais me cacher. "

Zufán se puso muy triste al darse cuenta de que había desobedecido a su papá y tenía mucho miedo de que la fuera a castigar. Zufán estaba en el jardín cuando vio un viejo armario vacío. Cuando Zufán lo vio, pensó "Ahí es donde me voy a esconder."

ዙፋን እሮጣ ቁም ሳጥኑ ውስጥ ገባች። በሩንም ዘግታ ጨለማው ውስጥ ተቀመጠች። ከትንሽ ጊዜም በኋላ በአካባቢው እንደሌለች ተገንዝበን ተደናገጥን።

Zufan ran over to the cupboard, climbed inside, and closed the door behind her, sitting in the dark. After a while everyone realized that they had not seen Zufan, and began to look for her.

Zufan couru vers le carton, grimpa à l'intérieur, ferma le dessus et s'assit dans l'obscurité. Après un certain temps, tout le monde se rendit compte que l'on avait plus vu Zefan et on commença à chercher après elle.

Zufán corrió al armario, se metió en él, cerró bien la puerta y se sentó en la oscuridad. Después de un rato todos se dieron cuenta de que no habían visto a Zufán y comenzaron a buscarla.

እናታችንና አጎታችን ዮሐንስም ፍለጋ ጀመሩ። እኛም "ዙፋን? እረ ዙፋን?" እያልን ጮህን። ዙፋን ግን አትመልስም። እናታችን በጣም ተሸበረች።

Her Mother and her Uncle Yohannes began to look for Zufan, and her sisters walked through the compound, calling out her name, but Zufan did not answer. After a while her mother began to get worried.

Sa mère et son oncle Yohannes commencèrent à chercher après Zefan et ses sœurs marchèrent à travers la propriété, appelant son nom. Mais Zufan ne répondit pas. Sa mère commença à s'inquiéter.

Su mamá y su tío Yohannes comenzaron a buscarla, y sus hermanas fueron por todos lados llamándola, pero Zufán no respondió. Entonces su mamá se comenzó a preocupar.

ሁላችንም ተጨንቀን ነበር። በይበልጥ የዙፋን ታላቅ እህት ፀጋ በጣም ተጨንቃ ነበር። “ዙፋን! አንቺ ዙፋን!” እያለች ትጮህ ነበር።

Zufan's sisters were all worried, and her older sister, Tsega, was particularly worried, so she kept walking through the courtyard yelling "Zufan, Here, Zufan!"

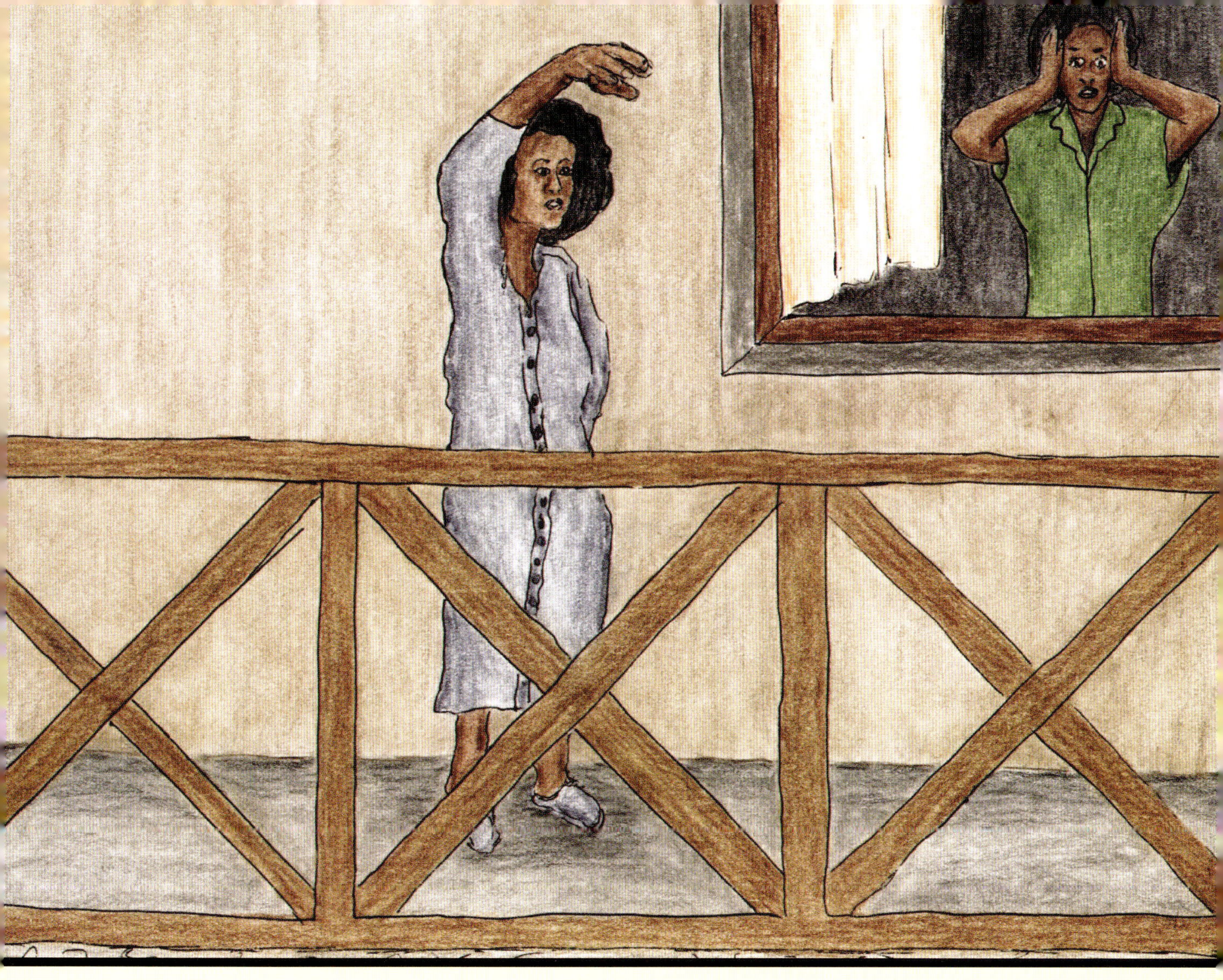

Les sœurs de Zufan étaient toutes très inquiètes et l'aînée, Tsega, continua à crier le nom de sa sœur : " Zufan, Zufan ! "

Las hermanas de Zufán estaban muy preocupadas, y sobretodo Tsega la hermana mayor estaba muy preocupada; ella continuó caminando por el jardín gritando "¡Zufán, dónde estás, Zufán!"

የዙፋን ታናሽ እህት ወሰንም መጨነቅ ብቻ ሳይሆን ፈርታም ነበር። "ዙፋንን ጅብ በልቷት ይሆን?" እያለች ማልቀስ ጀመረች። የሁላችንም ታላቅ ምርያም "ወሰን አታልቅሺ! ዙፋን ደህና ነች ብዬሻለሁ!" ስትል አባበለቻት።

Zufan's little sister, Wossen, was so scared and worried about Zufan she began to cry, worrying out loud, "Maybe a hyena has eaten her?" The oldest sister, Meriam, comforted her, saying "No, Wossen, don't cry. Zufan will be okay."

La petite sœur de Zufan, Wossen, eut tellement peur et était tellement inquiète pour sa sœur qu'elle commença à pleurer, disant : " Peut être qu'une hyène l'a mangée. " La sœur la plus âgée, Meriam, la réconforta en lui disant : " Non, ne t'en fais pas, Zufan va très bien. "

La hermanita más pequeña, Wossen, tenía tanto miedo y estaba tan preocupada que comenzó a llorar y a gritar en voz alta: "¡A lo mejor se la comió una hiena!". La hermana mayor de todas, Meriam, la trataba de tranquilizar diciéndole: "No, Wossen, no llores. Zufán está bien, ya verás."

ጊዜው ሲገፋም ዘመዶቻችንና ጎረቤቶቻችን ዙፋንን ለመፈለግ መጡ። አባታችንም ልጁ እንደጠፋች ተነግሮት ፍለጋውን ጀመረ። ቀኑም ሲጨልም ተዳከምን፡ ፍለጋችንን ግን አላቋረጥንም ነበር።

As time went on all of the neighbors and nearby relatives came to search for Zufan, and her father checked all the brush and bushes in the neighborhood looking for her. It began to get dark, and the people searching for Zufan were becoming exhausted, but they continued to look for her.

Comme le temps passait, les voisins et toute la famille se joignirent à la recherche de Zufan. Son père fouilla tous les arbustes et les buissons dans le voisinage en espérant trouver sa fille. La nuit commença à tomber et les gens cherchant Zufan étaient très fatigués. Mais ils continuèrent néanmoins.

Al pasar el tiempo, los vecinos y los familiares vinieron a buscar a Zufán y su papá revisó todos los arbustos de la vecindad. Cuando comenzó a oscurecer la gente buscando a Zufán estaba ya muy cansada pero todos continuaron buscándola.

ዙፋን ብዙ ሰው በጨለማ እየፈለጋት መሆኑን ምንም ሳይሰማት ፀጥ ብላ ተደብቃለች። ከጊዜም በኋላ በጨለማ መቀመጥ ሰለደከማትና በውጭ የሚሆነውን ማየት ሰለፈለገች በጭላንጭል ከቁም ሳጥኑ ውጭ ተመለከተች። ጫጫታውና ለቅሶው ስለጠነከረ የቁም ሳጥኑን በር ገርበብ አደረገችው።

Inside the cabinet Zufan could not really hear what was happening even though she was sitting very still and being quiet. Zufan finally got tired of sitting in the dark and wanted to see what was going on, so she peeked through a hole in the cupboard. Seeing the commotion and crying Zufan became curious, and opened the cupboard door just slightly so she could see and hear what was going on.

Dans sa cachette, Zufan ne pouvait rien entendre de ce qui se passait à l'extérieur. Elle était très silencieuse et ne bougeait pas dans son carton. Mais Zufan commençait à être fatiguée de rester assise tout le temps sans bouger et sans rien dire. Elle regarda donc à travers un trou dans le carton pour voir ce qui se passait à l'extérieur. Comme elle voyait ce qui se passait : les gens qui pleuraient et s'inquiétaient. Elle était curieuse de savoir ce qui se passait et décida de sortir de sa cachette.

Dentro del viejo armario, Zufán no sabía exactamente qué estaba pasando, aunque estaba muy quieta sin moverse. Por fin Zufán se cansó de estar sentada en la oscuridad y quiso ver qué estaba pasando, entonces se asomó por un pequeño agujero en el gabinete. Cuando vio la conmoción y escuchó los llantos, Zufán sintió curiosidad y abrió la puerta un poco para poder ver y oír lo que estaba pasando.

ከተሰበሰበው ሰው መሀል ሙሉጌታ የሚባል የሰፈራችን ልጅ ነበረ። ሙሉጌታ የቁም ሳጥኑ በር ሲንቀሳቀስ ተገነዘበ። ገርበብ ያለውን በር ሲመለከት የዙፋንን ፊት አየ። ወደ እናታችን እሮጦ ሄደ። እነደደረሰም "እማማ! እማማ! ዙፋንን አየኋት! ዙፋንን አገኘኋት!" ሲል ቁርጥ ቁርጥ ባለ ትንፋሽ ተናገረ።

One of the searchers in the courtyard was a neighborhood boy name Mulugetta. Mulugetta saw the cupboard door move, and then saw Zufan's face, so he ran to Zufan's mother, yelling as he ran. "Momma, Momma!" He shouted, "I found Zufan!"

Un des membres du groupe qui cherchait Zufan, était un petit garçon qui s'appelait Mulugetta. Mulugetta vit le dessus de la boîte de carton s'ouvrir et ensuite le visage de Zufan, donc il courut en direction de la mère de Zufan en criant : " Je l'ai trouvée, je l'ai trouvée. "

Una de las personas que ayudaban en la búsqueda en el jardín era un niño de los vecinos que se llamaba Mulugetta. Cuando Mulugetta vio la puerta del gabinete moverse y vio la cara de Zufán asomarse, corrió hacia la mamá de Zufán gritando: "¡Mamá, mamá, encontré a Zufán!"

ሙሉጌታን የሰሙ ሁሉ ተሰባሰቡ። “የት አገኘሃት? የት አየሃት?” እያሉም ደጋግመው ጠየቁት። እናታችንም “የት ነች? ልጄ የት ነች?” ብላ ጠየቀች። ሙሉጌታም በፈገግታ “እዚያ!...እዚያ ቁም ሳጥን ውስጥ ነች!” ሲል ጣቱን ወደ ቁም ሳጥኑ አቅጣጫ ጠቆመ።

Everyone gathered around Mulugetta and asked "Where, where?" Zufan's mother came over and asked him "Where is my child? Where is Zufan?" "Over there!" Mulugetta laughed and pointed at the old cupboard. "I saw her inside the cupboard!"

Tout le monde se rassembla autour de Mulugetta et demanda : " Où ? ". La mère de Zufan vint près de Mulugetta et lui demanda : " Où est Zufan ? Où est mon enfant ? " " Là-bas ! " Répondit Mulugetta en rigolant et en montrant la boîte de carton. " Je l'ai vue à l'intérieur de cette boîte en carton. "

Todos corrieron hacia Mulugetta y le preguntaron "¿Dónde, dónde?". La madre de Zufán se acercó y le preguntó "¿Dónde está mi niña? ¿Dónde está Zufán?". "¡Ahí!", Mulugetta se rió y señalando el viejo armario dijo: "¡Yo la vi adentro del armario!"

ሁላችንም ወደ ቁም ሳጥኑ አመራን እናታችንም የቁም ሳጥኑን በር ስትከፍት ልጇን አገኘቻት። አንስታም አቀፈቻት ደጋግማም ሳመቻት። በዚህም ጊዜ አባታችን ደረሰ፡ እጆቹንም ዘርግቶ “ ነይ የኔ ልጅ” አለ። እናታችንም በፈገግታ ዙፋንን ሰጠችው፡ አቅፎ ሳማትም።

Everyone went over to the cupboard, and her mother opened it to find Zufan inside, looking afraid and very tired. She pulled Zufan out of the cupboard, picked her up and hugged her, kissing her again and again. Zufan's father ran up to them, and held out his arms, saying "Come here, my little beauty." Her mother smiled, and handed Zufan to him, and he hugged and kissed her, too.

Tout le monde se dirigea vers la boîte de carton, et sa mère l'ouvrit pour découvrir Zufan à l'intérieur qui était fatiguée et apeurée. Elle prit Zufan dans ses bras et l'embrassa tendrement. Le père de Zufan accourut et tendit ses bras vers Zufan en lui disant : " Viens ici, ma petite beauté. " Sa mère sourit et lui tendit Zufan et son père l'embrassa aussi.

Todos se acercaron al armario, y su madre lo abrió por fin vio a Zufán dentro; se veía asustada y muy cansada. Ella sacó a Zufán del armario, la cargó y la abrazó, besándola una y otra vez. El padre de Zufán llegó corriendo hasta ellas, y le ofreció los brazos, diciéndole "¡Ven aquí, mi niña hermosa!". Su madre sonrió, y le entregó a Zufán a su padre quien también la abrazó y besó.

አባታችንም ትንሽ ፈገግ በማለት “ዙፋን ይቅር እልሻለሁ፡ ሁለትኛ አበባዎቹን አትንኪ። ከአበባውም የበለጠ ቤተሰቦችሽን አስደነገጥሽ። ሁለተኛ ለመደበቅ አትሞክሪ” የገባት ቆይቶ ቢሆንም ዙፋን በዚያን ዕለት ሁለት ነገሮችን ተምራለች፡ አንደኛ ምንም ብታጠፋም ወላጆቿ እንደሚወዷት አወቀች። ሁለተኛ ለመደበቅ መሞከር ነገሮችን እንደሚያበላሽም አወቀች።

Zufan's father smiled at her, and then told her "Zufan, I forgive you, but don't pull up the flowers again. But more important than the flowers, you scared your family. Don't ever run away." Although she would not really understand it until later, on that day Zufan learned two very important lessons. Zufan learned that her parents really loved her, no matter what she did, and that trying to run away from trouble only makes things worse.

Le père de Zufan lui sourit et lui dit : " Zefan, je te pardonne mais ne cueille plus jamais aucune fleur de ce jardin. Mais ce qui est encore plus important que les fleurs est que tu as effrayé toute ta famille et tes amis. Ne fugue plus jamais ! " Malgré que Zufan n'était pas encore assez âgée pour comprendre cela, elle découvrira plus tard qu'elle a apprit deux leçons importantes ce jour-là : que ses parents l'adorent plus que tout et que essayer de s'enfuir et d'éviter les problèmes ne fait que les empirer.

El padre de Zufán sonrió, y luego le dijo: "Zufán, te perdono, pero no vuelvas a cortar las flores. Pero más importante que la flor, es que asustaste a la familia. Nunca vuelvas a escaparte". Aunque ella realmente no lo entendería hasta más tarde, aquel día Zufán aprendió dos lecciones muy importantes: Zufán aprendió que sus padres realmente la aman, pase lo que pase y haga lo que haga y que el intentar escaparse de un problema sólo empeora las cosas.

THE END